Contemplating Craft Freemasonry

CONTEMPLATING CRAFT FREEMASONRY

Working the
Way of the Craftsman

W. Kirk MacNulty

WASHINGTON, D.C.

In the Year of Light 6018

http://www.plumbstone.com

Cover: *Study for Novum Rose* by Ryan J. Flynn, www.ryanjflynn.com.

Publisher's Cataloging-in-Publication Data

Contemplating craft freemasonry: working the way of the craftsman / W. Kirk MacNulty.

    103 p. 25 cm.
    ISBN 978-1-60302-024-4 (pbk)
    ISBN 978-1-60302-025-1 (ebook)
    1. Freemasonry—Symbolism. 2. Freemasonry—Ritual.
    3. Mysticism. 4. Hermetism. 5. Cabala.
    I. MacNulty, W. Kirk, 1932–, author. II. Eyer, Shawn, foreword.
    III. Compton, Spencer, Lord Northampton, 1946–, foreword.
    SOCIAL SCIENCE / Freemasonry & Secret Societies.
    RELIGION / Mysticism.
    HS425 .M31 89 2017 (print) 366´.1—dc23.

Library of Congress Control Number: 2018936835

Dedication

To all poor and distressed Masons
wherever dispersed
over the face of Earth and Water;

Wishing them a speedy relief
from all their suffering,

And a safe return
to their native country
should they so desire it.

Everything in Masonry has reference to God,
implies God, speaks of God, points and leads to
God. Not a degree, not a symbol, not an obligation,
not a lecture, not a charge but finds its meaning and
derives its beauty from God, the Great Architect,
in whose temple all Masons are workmen.

—Joseph Fort Newton

Contents

Foreword

I take pleasure in writing a brief foreword for Kirk MacNulty's latest work on Freemasonry. For me, the Craft degrees are a journey towards Truth, our third Grand Principle. A journey leading to integration which begins in earnest the moment we are initiated into a lodge and brings us to an understanding of the interconnectedness of all life. It is refreshing to find such profound truths explained in a way which can be readily understood by Masons and non-Masons alike.

Kirk has given the reader much to contemplate and I personally have made many new discoveries. These have, without doubt, enriched my Masonic experience and I commend this book to all seekers after Truth.

> Lord Northampton
> Pro Grand Master (2001–2009)
> United Grand Lodge of England

Publisher's Foreword

In 1772, the Lodge of Antiquity—one of the four original lodges that formed the Grand Lodge of England in 1717—hosted a Grand Gala for the leadership of the Fraternity at the Crown and Anchor Tavern in the Strand, London. During this event, the first performance of William Preston's beautiful lecture of the first degree was performed. In his address at the beginning of the Gala, Brother Preston presented his perspective on Freemasonry as a speculative science:

> Speculative Masonry is so much interwoven with religion, as to lay us under the strongest obligations to pay to the Deity that rational homage, which at once constitutes the duty and happiness of mankind. It leads the contemplative to view with reverence and admiration the glorious works of the creation, and inspires them with the most exalted ideas of the perfections of the great Creator.[1]

The work was the result of a careful process of the curation of Masonic tradition, benefiting from interviews with elderly brethren, many of whom would have been initially active during the early years of the Grand Lodge. Preston's youth—he was twenty-nine years of age at the time—proved no impediment to the acceptance of his project. The Grand Lodge leadership endorsed his work and encouraged him to continue developing lectures for the other Masonic degrees. Preston published some of what took place at the Gala in the first edition of his influential masterpiece, *Illustrations of Masonry*, in which he included a Eulogium that concluded:

1   William Preston, *Illustrations of Masonry* (London: J. Williams, 1772), 12-13.

Such are the general advantages of Masonry; to enumerate them separately, would be an endless labour: suffice it to say, that he who is possest of this true science, and acts agreeably to the character he bears, has within himself the spring and support of every social virtue; a subject of contemplation that enlarges the mind, and expands every mental power; a subject that is inexhaustible, is ever new, and always interesting.[2]

Preston was surely not the first to advocate a contemplative approach to Freemasonry, but his lectures make the role of active intellectual engagement absolutely central for a proper understanding of the Craft. And, since Preston's language is so pervasive within both the common American workings and the English Emulation Rite and its variants, that emphasis on authentic contemplation as a key to getting the most out of the Craft will always be an integral part of regular Freemasonry.

When Plumbstone began publishing Masonic books over ten years ago, the first releases were annotated versions of works by W.L. Wilmshurst. Wilmshurst—like William Preston centuries before him—saw Freemasonry as a profound system of initiation worthy of deep contemplation. The vision that he espoused in his books, *The Meaning of Masonry* and *The Masonic Initiation*, inspired the creation of The Lodge of Living Stones № 4957 in England, and, later, the Traditional Observance lodges of North America.

It was within Wilmshurst's Lodge of Living Stones that Brother W. Kirk MacNulty developed many of the ideas expressed in his books. Later, he brought these understandings to America, where he became the Charter Master of The Lodge of the Nine Muses № 1776 in Washington, D.C. As one who has enjoyed the insights from Brother MacNulty's writings, it has been a pleasure

2   Preston, *Illustrations* (1772), 186–87.

for me to serve this lodge as Junior Warden for several years. To work within a lodge that encourages the contemplation of the mysteries of Masonry is a tremendous privilege.

Our founding Master's works are extremely valuable to any who wish to understand Freemasonry more fully. His beautiful and lavishly-illustrated books published by Thames and Hudson— *Freemasonry: A Journey Through Ritual and Symbol* (1991), and *Freemasonry: Symbols, Secrets, Significance* (2006)—belong on every Mason's bookshelf. And he is best known for *The Way of the Craftsman: A Search for the Spiritual Essence of Craft Freemasonry*, which first appeared in 1988 and is now available in a deluxe edition from Plumbstone.

Whether we reflect back upon William Preston's Masonry of the eighteenth century or on W.L. Wilmshurst's fraternity of the 1920s, it is clear that the need for us to actively pursue Masonic Light if we wish to truly participate in whole of our degree work is unchanged.

We can chose to be contemplative Masons or not. It is possible to simply carry a membership card and pass while wearing the Masonic apron as a kind of friendly (if somewhat cynical) disguise. But our speculative Art calls us to more. The process of initiation demands our sincere engagement if it is to be truly effective. Masonic readers can indeed be truly grateful for authors such as W. Kirk MacNulty, who have done so much to provide new opportunities to gain a deeper understanding of the degrees as they share the ideas that helped them along their respective journeys.

Shawn Eyer
Alexandria, Virginia

Preface

In March 2009, *Freemasonry Today* published an interview with Lord Northampton, then the Pro Grand Master of the United Grand Lodge of England. The Editor who interviewed him said:

> Lord Northampton has helped usher in a new way of defending and advancing Freemasonry ... augmenting the experience of its ritual and the understanding of its profound philosophical side which arise from the deepest meaning of those central Masonic principles, Brotherly Love, Relief and Truth.

Lord Northampton then went on to say:

> The idea of "becoming a Freemason" is something of a misnomer. I think that you are born a Freemason. There is something within you which leads you to want to develop in an integrated way, to seek self-development to become a better person. And part of this search involves considering the major questions about life and death. You should join Freemasonry if you are looking for moral and spiritual values in a world which is predominantly focused upon material concerns.
>
> Absolute truth is outside time and place; it is a constant from which all things flow. This has to be the highest state of integrity possible. We can best explain this symbolically and one very good symbol is that of Jacob's Ladder which is depicted on the First Degree tracing board. This ladder reaches from earth to heaven; as you climb higher on the ladder you can see further. You can see how you are connected with, and contribute to, the whole, you can see that integrity, truth and freedom are all connected.

About that time, Lord Northampton asked me if I would prepare a series of short papers or talks that Masters of Lodges could read and discuss within their Lodges, in order to explain and inculcate the philosophical ideas—especially those related to Truth—as most Freemasons focus on Brotherly Love and Relief.

This book provides a compilation of those short talks, augmented with several others, so that the reader may obtain a more comprehensive picture of what a Masonic Lodge is and can be, from this philosophical perspective.

The book can be used in two ways—one as Lord Northampton suggested, with readings of the talks by the Master, followed by discussion—and the other as a study plan for personal growth, with the chapters to be read, studied and acted upon by the individual Freemason. Indeed, in both cases, much value can be obtained by reading the chapters as lessons to be learned and then experienced in daily life.

For instance, as part of the discussion in the Lodge, the Master could ask "What does this chapter mean in daily life?" If it is a chapter about a Working Tool, then "How can this Tool be applied?" If it is a chapter about a symbol, then "What does this symbol mean in one's daily life?" The Master could assign "homework" in which he asks the members to apply and experience the Tool/Symbol over the course of the weeks before the next Lodge meeting. Then, when the Lodge reconvenes, he could ask what each member has experienced. In that way, a Masonic Lodge can become a Working Group, benefiting its members in ways that go beyond the usual meetings and ceremonies. Examples of such questions are given at the end of each chapter.

So why did I think that this would be a good idea? And why have I turned these papers into a book?

I became a Freemason in 1961 while living in Gardnerville, Nevada. It was a small country town, with a Masonic Lodge and a dedicated group of members. As I went through the ritual of the third degree, I had some profound insights about my own life, the meaning of life, and the meaning of Freemasonry. That started me on a quest to learn more, to know more, and to communicate to others a real and deeper meaning of Masonry than many of its members are aware. Then, while living in London, I had the opportunity to get to know Lord Northampton, John Hamill, and other luminaries of the United Grand Lodge of England, and they encouraged me in my Masonic writing.

In addition, I have run, and participated in, Masonic Study groups both in the United States and the United Kingdom, and have gained enormous insight into my own life, as well as a deeper understanding of the nature of the Craft. The views expressed in this book are my own, and are not necessarily those of any Grand Lodge.

I believe that there is much to be learned about life from the study and practice of Freemasonry, and I hope that you, the reader, will find it to be as rewarding as I have.

W. Kirk MacNulty
Arlington, Virginia

UNDERSTANDING THE ESSENCE OF CRAFT FREEMASONRY

In this introduction, we will consider our working in Freemasonry in a manner that is rather different than usual. We will ask ourselves, "Why are we here? What is the purpose of the Craft?" While many believe that the answers to those questions are fairly obvious, it is the author's hope that this section will introduce some new thoughts.

The basic principles of Freemasonry are "Brotherly Love, Relief, and Truth." When it comes to Brotherly Love, it is reasonable to argue that our Fraternity is doing pretty well. Our lodges are places of good fellowship where friendship and rewarding social interactions are easy and gratifying. Without doubt, it should be our endeavor to ensure that that situation continues. On the subject of Relief we are doing even better. Masonic charities are noted for their generous giving to society in general, as well as to Brother Masons; and our Order receives much gratitude—from Masons and from non-Masons—for these gifts. We should work in this area, too, to ensure that we continue in this way. Truth is, perhaps, a bit more of a puzzle. Certainly, we are truthful with each other and with the world; but that seems to be little more than the behavior of most people in our society. Why do we need our elaborate rituals to teach that, or does Truth in the Masonic context mean something else?

So, why are we here? Well, our teachings are very clear on that subject. It is work of the Craft to "make good men better." And, of course, we do that. In our lodges, we teach the principles of the proper behavior and the morality which are the very foundation of our culture. But there is a puzzle here. Imagine a meeting of this lodge at which a man is to be proposed as a candidate. Let us consider what would be likely to transpire if, immediately prior to the ballot, one of our brethren rose and said, "My brothers, I am sorry to have to say this, but this man who seeks to become a candidate for our Brotherhood is actually known to me to be a thief. He has embezzled thousands of dollars from a private trust of which he is the trustee." It is almost certain that, under these circumstances, when the revelation was verified, more than one of the brethren present would place a black ball into the ballot box. The same thing should happen if the prospective candidate were revealed to be a chronic liar, a child abuser, or a perpetrator of any other serious offence. Why have I made this digression about ballots? Because it points out that we already do our best to admit to membership only those men who are practicing the very principles of morality that we teach. So what are we really doing and teaching to "make good men better?" That seems to be a puzzle, too.

Is it possible that these two puzzling situations are interrelated? I think they are. It is the Truth that we should be teaching to "make good men better." So what is the Truth in that context? Within the principle of Truth is contained the notion of the profound philosophical wisdom that is the basis of our understanding of reality. We do not seem to be giving that idea much attention. Is there some way to understand Freemasonry that will enable us to understand Truth in a different way, and thus, to teach it? I think there is, and we must examine the development of the Order carefully in order to understand it in that context. Since Freemasonry, as we understand it today, is observable first at the end of the Renaissance, let us start our examination by observing the ideas of that period. During the Middle Ages, the thrust of intellectual activity had been to reconcile the writings of the classical philosophers with the doctrines of Christianity. The purpose of human life was to ensure the salvation of one's soul after death. Innovative ideas were not desired, and the epistemology was authoritarian. If one wanted to know something, one asked the Church. In the latter half of the fourteenth century, a group of scholars in Florence, Italy, began to study the classical philosophers simply to learn what they had said about mankind. It should be no surprise, therefore, that classical ideas are to be found in the thinking of the Renaissance.

By the middle of the fifteenth century, the emerging Renaissance was supported by the Medici family which was patron of a Neoplatonic school in Florence. Two important philosophical disciplines found their way to this school. The first was the *Corpus Hermeticum*.[1] Marcilio Ficino, who was translating the text, took it to be the work of the book's principal character, Hermes Trismegistus, whom Ficino took to be an Egyptian contemporary of Moses. That assumption (which was later shown to be incorrect) made the *Hermetica* appear to be something approaching a pagan prophesy of Christianity, and that made

1   See my earlier work, *The Way of the Craftsman: Deluxe Edition* (Plumbstone, 2017), pp. 12–14, for more details.

its study acceptable to the Church. The second philosophical discipline was Kabbalah, the mystical tradition of Judaism. During the Moorish occupation of Spain Sufis, Kabbalists, and Christian mystics had thrived. They had worked together, and a substantial amount of literature had been produced. With the Christian reconquest of Spain in the late fifteenth century, a large amount of kabbalistic literature found its way to Florence, where it was translated and interpreted by Pico della Mirandola. From this intellectual environment there emerged what Dame Frances A. Yates has called the Hermetic-kabbalistic tradition that was to become the philosophical essence of the Renaissance.

How does all of this relate to Freemasonry? The earliest evidence of Masonic activity in the context that we understand the Order today occurs in Northern England in the mid-to-late seventeenth century. That is the time of the end of the Renaissance in Britain and Northern Europe. Let us consider the major metaphysical principles of the Renaissance philosophy and see how they can be related to Freemasonry. In general, there are four such principles. The first principle is Neoplatonism, an idea that was developed in Alexandria in the third century. Since a creator must be separate from his creation, the description of "creation" in Genesis implies a limited Deity. The idea behind Neoplatonism says that the Deity, which is beyond existence, wills itself into existence as All that Is. This seems, at first, to be an unusual idea, but it was not unpopular. St. Augustine of Hippo, one of the Fathers of the Church, was a strong supporter of Neoplatonism. When examined closely, it appears to support many Christian teachings. Certainly it is consistent with the other principles we will examine.

The second principle is that of a macrocosm and a microcosm. The macrocosm is the universe; the microcosm is mankind. Both are said to have been made in the image of God, and the same laws are said to operate for both. The third principle is that the Universe consists of four levels: the *physical* level; the *celestial* (psychological) level; the *super-celestial* (spiritual) level; and the *divine* level. This terminology was devised at a time when the universe was thought to be geocentric, and the planets and stars were thought to be the agencies through which the Deity acted in the world. Today these levels can be understood as the physical level, the psychological level, the spiritual level, and divinity. Opposites are held in balance at each level. This idea is presented in the Tree of Life, a principal kabbalistic device, which is shown on the next page. That diagram can be used to represent any open system; as shown here, it represents the entire Universe. There are three columns. The one on the right is the column of mercy, and it contains all the active principles and powers. The one of the left is the column of severity, and it contains all the constraining principles and powers. The column of consciousness is in the center, and it holds the active and constraining forces in balance. The central column is also considered by kabbalists to be a ladder of consciousness which one climbs. The four levels are indicated on the diagram by the overlapping circles, that of divinity being open to indicate that this level is without limitation.

The fourth principle is the idea of the mystical ascent, a central idea of the Renaissance. The philosophers of the Renaissance who embraced these ideas were devout Christians, some even clergy; and they certainly aspired to salvation after death. However, they believed that by serious practice of the principles of their faith they could rise from the physical world, through the levels of the psyche and the spirit, and experience the divine presence here and now, while they were incarnate. Indeed, this idea is to be found in all the great religions—although in many, it is not widely acknowledged.

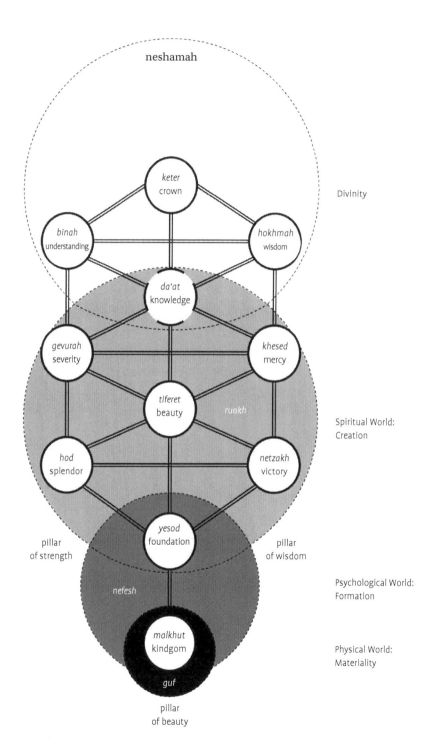

The lodge degrees are three mystical dramas which describe the progress through these levels of consciousness. Simply experiencing the degrees does not ensure that one rises through those levels in fact. To rise through the levels after one has received the degrees one must live the experiences in practice, a process which one must do one's self and which can take many years.

Now let us look at the symbolic structure of Freemasonry, and see if these ideas can be found there. I must acknowledge that this interpretation of Masonic symbolism is that of the author of this paper. However, the correspondence between the three columns on the first degree tracing board (shown on page 9), the three upper levels of the Tree of Life, and the three degrees of Freemasonry, seem to me to be very significant. Indeed, they offer an interpretation of the degrees in the context of a developmental psychology. I have explored this subject more thoroughly in the books listed at the end of this volume.

Periodically during this examination, we will refer to King Solomon's Temple. We will consider that structure in the context provided in the Great Light, where we are profoundly asked: "Know ye not that ye are the temple?" Both the Lodge and the Temple that it represents are models of the individual Freemason.

Understanding the First Degree

We will start with the tracing board of the first degree which is shown on page 9. The first of the principles is Neoplatonism—the Deity willing itself into existence. I suggest that this is represented on the tracing board by the Ornaments of the Lodge: Blazing Star or Glory, the Checkered Pavement, and the Tessellated Border. Together, these three Ornaments communicate the Law of Unity.

The Blazing Star or Glory is not what a contemporary astronomer would call a "stellar object." After all, stellar objects are to be found around the moon in the upper right of the Board. The Blazing Star is a straightforward heraldic representation of the Deity as It is, at the moment that It wills Itself into existence. The Checkered Pavement is a representation of the Deity as It is perceived at the opposite pole of consciousness, in the physical world. The black and white squares represent paired opposites, hot and cold, easy and difficult, happy and sad, etc. But the squares as such are not the symbol. The Pavement is the symbol. All the squares fit together with precision to form the Pavement, which is shown to be without limit. The Border, here around the whole picture, binds all into a single unity; and the Tassels represent the omnipresence of the Deity.

The idea of duality is to be found throughout the Board, from the Pavement at the bottom to the Sun and Moon—classical symbols of male and female—in the Heavens. In the central part of the Board, where most of the Masonic symbols are to be found, this duality is represented by the Doric and Corinthian Columns. The Doric Column, plain and severe, represents Strength, while the Corinthian Column, vibrant and beautiful, represents Beauty. But here the Ionic Column, between the other two and representing Wisdom, introduces the idea of a third agency that holds opposites in balance. The roles of the Officers of the Lodge to which those Columns relate support that idea. There are four levels shown on the tracing board. The Pavement represents the Physical World; the central part, the area containing most of the Masonic Symbols, represents the Psyche; the Heavens represent the Spirit; and, as we have seen, the Blazing Star represents divinity.

The symbols we have considered thus far represent the Macrocosm, or the Universe. Where is the Microcosm, or man? One

of the most prominent symbols on the Board is Jacob's Ladder, which we will consider together with the Point Within a Circle Bounded by Two Parallel Lines. We will consider these two symbols together because they are frequently found together in Masonic drawings.

The Two Parallel Lines traditionally represent the Holy Saints John: St. John the Baptist and St. John the Evangelist. After the 1813 Union of the Antients and the Moderns in England, the new United Grand Lodge of England promoted an alternative correspondence for the line, referring them respectively to Moses the Prophet and Solomon the Lawgiver. In American lodges, the ancient symbolism of the Holy Saints John remains intact. It is interesting to note that, in both the traditional version retained in the United States and in the reformed English version, the two Biblical figures associated with the Parallel Lines may be reasonably understood as representing opposite personalities.

Since the Baptist's Day is mid-summer and the Evangelist's Day is mid-winter, it seems clear that the intent is that these Lines should represent paired opposites. Between the lines we find Jacob's Ladder which rises through the three levels of Faith, Hope, and Charity to the fourth level of divinity. Notice the points of the compass on the border of the board. East is at the top, and West is at the bottom. Now, one of the lectures speaks of Freemasons traveling to the "East in search of instruction." That lecture and tracing board together certainly suggest that the climbing of this ladder is a representation of the fourth metaphysical principle, the mystical ascent.

The Entered Apprentice degree is said to take place—and the Apprentice is said to work—on the Ground Floor of King Solomon's Temple; and there are several important lessons to be learned there. For example: The candidate crosses a threshold and enters a new environment, the Lodge. The candidate must leave behind certain things, things that will speak of his power and status in the ordinary world. This teaches us that the individual must leave behind the things of "this world," while he is studying the interior work. The Working Tools of the Degree are tools of action. They can be understood to represent the candidate's capacities for passion—the Gavel, for analysis—the Chisel, and for the ability to determine how much of each and when to apply it—the Gauge. The candidate is told to practice the Cardinal Virtues; and if he does so, he will certainly establish a calm and stable life. Such a life will enable him to undertake the interior work necessary for the mystical ascent without distracting interruptions. Secrecy is an important lesson of the Entered Apprentice degree, and that is certainly a principle to be applied by those doing the interior work of that Ascent. While doing that interior work one learns very personal things which should not be shared with people who cannot understand them. As one of the most revered teachers in the history of Western Civilization once said, "neither cast ye your pearls before swine." That is the lesson of the symbol of secrecy.

The Junior Warden is the officer who presides over the Ground Floor of Solomon's Temple. When the Temple is understood to be a model of the individual Freemason, the Ground Floor might be seem as representing the level of consciousness in the ordinary world. To use contemporary terminology, the final objective of labor in the first degree is the individuation of the Self. As the term is used in Jungian psychology, the Self represents the whole of the personality, both conscious and subconscious, and is distinct from the ego.[2] The Junior Warden represents the

---

2   In 1955, Jung wrote: "I have defined the self as the totality of the conscious and unconscious psyche, and the ego as the central reference-point of consciousness." See *Mysterium Coniunctionis* (Princeton, N.J.: Princeton University Press, 1963), 110. Jungians often capitalize the word Self in order to make it clear that they are referring to this special definition of the word in the context of depth psychology.

Self. When a person has achieved a mature and self-possessed state of consciousness, he is most ready for the second degree. Of course, a candidate can refuse some of these opportunities—in which case the he can practice the activities of good fellowship, but the process of interior growth fails.

Understanding the Second Degree

The tracing board of the second degree (shown on page 13) contains a symbolic structure that should be, by now, quite familiar. There are two Columns, topped with the Celestial and Terrestrial Spheres. These certainly represent two opposite verticals, and between them there is the ladder, which has become a staircase.

There are also four levels in the picture: the Ground Floor, the Middle Chamber to which the stairs lead, the blue balcony representing the spirit, and the sun-like luminary. The sun cannot shine inside a building—as such, I think that the luminary is a representation of the Blazing Star or Glory, which is to say it represents the presence of the divinity. In addition, the Temple is depicted here in the context of St. Paul's profound question, "Know ye not that ye are the temple of God, and that the Spirit of God dwelleth in you?" (1 Corinthians 3:16) When the Temple is viewed as a symbol of the individual Freemason, the climbing of the stairs leading upward to the divine Glory suggests an *interior* ascent to higher levels of consciousness.

Although the second degree sometimes receives a relatively small amount of attention, I believe that the most important Masonic labor is to be conducted here. There are many important lessons taught on the Winding Stairs and in the Middle Chamber. Let us look first at the lessons on the Ground Floor and

the Stairs. Outside the Temple there is an Ear of Corn growing next to the waterfall. It suggests that the process we are about to examine is one of natural growth and maturation. The bottom of the Winding Stairs is guarded by the Junior Warden, whom we have already identified with the "Self." His presence there suggests that the "Self" must individuate before the interior ascent can be started.

The Junior Warden stands guard and will only admit the candidate to the Middle Chamber when certain tests are answered correctly. The Hebrew word he expects is associated with a long and complex story which we will not examine here. The thing we should note is that the story associated with the password communicates two important lessons. Those lessons are: first, that one should not seek to undertake the interior ascent unless one has fulfilled the necessary prerequisites; and second, that if one seeks to climb one should be sure that he has the proper motive. I think this is a symbolic teaching of the idea expressed by Brother Elias Ashmole when he made the distinction between "true magicians" and "necromancers and witches."[3]

The climbing of the stairs is not usually considered to be a difficult adventure. However, in the context we are considering it involves learning a great deal about one's self; and that can sometime be a quite painful experience. In practice, the sharing of a difficult experience with an understanding Brother can be very helpful. It is for this reason that Masons are pledged to keep one another's secrets as their own, "murder, treason, and all other violations of the laws of God and the ordinances of the Realm at all times specifically excepted." The fact that "climbing the stairs" can be a stressful experience explains another aspect

3   See Elias Ashmole, *Theatrum Chemicum Britannicum: Containing Severall Poeticall Pieces of our Famous English Philosophers, Who Have Written the Hermetique Mysteries in their owne Ancient Language* (London: J. Grismond, 1652), 443.

of Freemasonry that many people find puzzling. One should never be talked into to undertaking the interior ascent. One must choose to do it for one's self. That is why each candidate must explicitly ask to join the Order.

At the top of the staircase in this picture, we see the Middle Chamber. Reaching that Chamber is not the culmination of the interior ascent, but it represents an important step where significant events occur. From the traditional perspective that "ye are the Temple," the Middle Chamber can be understood to represent the individual's soul; and that makes it a very significant area. The soul is the "principal organ" of the psyche; and in that respect it is the seat of the individual's morality. The working tools of the Fellow Craft degree reflect the individual's capacity for moral decision making. Unlike the Entered Apprentice's tools, which are tools of action, these are tools of testing. Each tool tests against an absolute criterion, two of those criteria are opposite, and the third defines the relationship between the other two.

I associate the Plumbrule with license and allowing and the Level with prudence and restraint. The Square keeps them in balance. The Perfect Ashlar also contributes to this process. We are told that the Perfect Ashlar is in the Middle Chamber "for the experienced Craftsman to try his tools on," as some rituals instruct us. This is an interesting image from the operative craft. The squares, levels, and plumbs of the operative masons were usually made of wood—and when used on stones, they were gradually worn away. In the operative lodge on the building site there was a perfect stone to enable the craftsman to recalibrate his tools. When this symbolic image is applied to the specula-tive Fellow Craft in the Middle Chamber of his soul, it makes the Perfect Ashlar a good representation of one's conscience which enables one to calibrate the principles of one's morality.

The ritual tells us that the Craftsmen at Solomon's Temple

went to the Middle Chamber to receive their wages which were a fair reward for the work that had been done. When we look at the Middle Chamber as one's Soul, the symbol of Wages suggests that there is an agency within each individual that ensures he receives exactly that which he has earned. For some this can be an unsettling idea, particularly for those who are unhappy with their experiences. Viewed objectively, however, this is the very source of individual freedom. If one does not like one's wages (experience), one can do differently; and one will receive different wages (experience). This is a very old teaching. One of the earliest traditional expressions of the idea is found in the Volume of Sacred Law: "As a man soweth, so shall he reap."

Perhaps the most significant symbol in the Middle Chamber is the "Letter G." It is said to refer to Geometry, a "regular progression of science from a point to a line, from a line to a superficies, from a superficies to a solid." This definition touches only on a tiny aspect of Geometry, but the "Letter G" is generally thought also to be a symbolic reference to divinity. Since Geometry is the foundation of mathematics and enables us to think about the universe, it leads us to contemplation of the Deity. We should also note that science, as we understand it today, did not come into existence until the beginning of the nineteenth century. To the brethren who were establishing our Order, the word science denoted "knowledge acquired by study,"[4] rather than the practice of experimental science as it is commonly used today. The geometric progression is defined by Proclus, the last classical Neoplatonist, who was, of course, referenced in *A Defense of Masonry* in 1730. The same progression was used by Solomon ibn Gabirol in the eleventh century to describe the Neoplatonic progression of the Deity into existence.

In the broadest sense, the Middle Chamber of one's soul is

4   *Oxford English Dictionary.*

a place of contemplation. When one turns within, climbs one's Winding Stairs, and enters one's Middle Chamber to sit quietly and contemplate one's symbolic wages, as well as the Perfect Ashlar, the Letter G, and the things that those symbols imply, one is led sooner or later to the Holy of Holies in the Temple that one is.

Understanding the Third Degree

The tracing board of the third degree is illustrated on page 19. Clearly, the Emblems of Mortality gathered in this illustration inspire due and serious reflection. Unfortunately, the death described in the Master Mason's ritual is one of the most misunderstood aspects of Freemasonry.

The *nature* of that death, the reason why it is to be considered, and the implications of the event are of particular interest to us here. One of the central objects on the tracing board is King Solomon's Porch, the entrance to the Holy of Holies, and the curtain of that entrance is drawn back so that the Ark of the Covenant is visible. Each Master Mason has been in a ritual representation of this place, and at the time he was wearing the Jewel of the Junior Warden. This moment of ritual can be understood, I suggest, as the moment when one's contemplations lead one to the Holy of Holies in the Temple that one is.

But there is a problem here. The Holy of Holies is the place in the Temple where the Deity resides, and the Deity is without limit. If one becomes conscious of the presence of a Being that is without limit, one cannot exist as an independent entity. One dies. It is not a physical death. One's identity is not lost. It is the death of one's concept of one's "self."

This is a difficult idea to grasp, but it is described well by W. Bro. W. L. Wilmshurst, in his enduring classic, *The Meaning of Masonry*:

> Hence the third degree is that of mystical death, of which bodily death is taken as figurative, just as bodily birth is taken in the first degree as figurative of entrance upon the path of regeneration. In all the mystery systems of the past will be found this degree of mystical death as an outstanding and essential feature prior to the final stage of perfection or regeneration.[5]

Through this "mystical death" one is raised to a higher level of consciousness, I believe it to be consciousness at the level of the spirit; and at this level one can experience the divine Presence. Viewed from this perspective the death in the third degree is a form of *apotheosis.*

Notice the Points of the Compass on the third degree tracing board. The West, which was at the bottom of the first degree board, is now at the top of this board. This seems to indicate that the Brother who has had this experience now travels "West"—to the place from which he has grown—to spread the love and wisdom he has gained.

This degree is Freemasonry's most vivid representation of the mystical ascent, and it is a representation of one's search for authentic and immutable Truth. This idea of Truth cannot be communicated by words or in a lodge room by means of ritualistic dramas. The knowledge of Truth is an interior experience that must take place within each individual. Few experience it, because few understand the possibility—and among those that do, few follow the task with the persistence and sincerity that

5 W. L. Wilmshurst, *The Meaning of Masonry* (San Francisco, Calif.: Plumbstone, 2008), 98.

is required. Nonetheless, for those brethren who are interested in Truth, Freemasonry can be understood, and applied, as an instrument of the interior work.

It is the most profound way to "make good men better."

CONTEMPLATING THE WAY OF THE APPRENTICE

THE FIRST DEGREE IN PRACTICE

When a candidate knocks on the door of a Masonic Lodge he is standing, symbolically, at the threshold of his own consciousness. Beyond the door of the Lodge, the threshold of his consciousness, the candidate finds a "Temple," which is said to have four levels—a Ground Floor, a Middle Chamber, a Holy of Holies and, residing within this, the divine Presence.

According to Masonic traditions the three degrees are thought to take place in King Solomon's Temple; the first degree takes place on the Ground Floor. A new Mason, one who has just received the first degree, will have to become familiar with many Masonic symbols, and one of them is the Rough Ashlar. An ashlar in its rough state is a stone which has just been cut from the quarry, and it has not yet been shaped to fit as a building stone in the Temple. In a similar manner, the newly-initiated candidate has not yet learned the lessons which will guide him on his Masonic development.

The information for this growth is communicated, in part, in the lectures of the degree. The Working Tools of the first degree are tools of ACTION; of passion, analysis, balance; and the use of them can be very helpful.

In addition to the Working Tools, the candidate will have, in his own psyche, much material which will be very valuable. In participating in the ceremony, the candidate receives, symbolically, a perspective into the nature of his own psyche. For instance, the Working Tools may be viewed as relating to specific aspects of the psyche, and as providing instructions for their use.

If the candidate gives serious attention to these lessons and the work of the Lodge, and begins to understand it, there will come a moment when it all comes together, and he sees his psyche, his inner being, as represented by the symbolism. When he has such a real "Aha!" moment, and sees himself as an individual with specific characteristics, who can take control of his tendencies and can work to achieve specific capabilities, then he realizes that the thoughts he thinks and the decisions that he makes have real tangible effects on his own life and the lives of others. When he has had even a glimpse of the workings of his psyche, he can never forget it, he can never "unsee" it. Someone with this kind of thought will be more of an individual than many around him; he will know his own mind and his tendencies, and will be more likely to take responsibility for his actions and the situations in which he finds himself.

The material that is provided in the first degree encourages the candidate to take such a deep look at himself and the workings of his psyche, and this is one of the reasons that one must ask to become a Mason. No one should be asked to assume that sort of responsibility until he feels ready for it. This is only the start.

Individual responsibility for one's actions is a concept that will be developed as the candidate progresses through the degree.

ONE

The First Immovable Jewel: The Rough Ashlar

As mentioned in the previous section, an Ashlar is a stone which has been cut from the quarry, shaped to fit into the building for which it is intended, and ready for use. A Rough Ashlar is a stone cut from the quarry, but in no way shaped. It is not ready for any use at all; except that it can be shaped, with proper care and activity, into a stone that can be used in the Temple being built.

The very newly initiated Entered Apprentice Mason is associated with a Rough Ashlar cut from the bedrock because he has virtually no Masonic experience; and that reference will indicate his need to accumulate Masonic learning. In human terms it represents an individual human being who is becoming separate from the mass of humanity of which he was originally a part. In that state, as part of the bedrock, as a member of a group or society, with no personal control over his circumstances, he flows with that group or society; depends upon it for support, and takes its values as his own; and the experiences of his life are those of the members of society.

In participating in the ceremony of the first degree, the candidate receives, symbolically, insights into the nature of his own unique psyche, with the wise brethren, particularly those associated with the administration of the lodge, giving their attention to his Masonic education. Once he has had such insights and real (not symbolic) experiences that indicate that he is indeed an individual, which proves to him that the thoughts he thinks and the decisions he takes have a real, tangible and frequently immediate effect on his life and the lives of others, he can never forget it. And, just as the Rough Ashlar, which has been cut from the quarry, will thereafter be an individual stone, such a person will be an individual with individual responsibility for his actions and for the situations in which he finds himself for as long as he lives.

CONTEMPLATIONS

- So what are the implications of this chapter for your daily life?
- If you have been through the Ceremony of the first degree, even if it was many years ago, what did you learn?
- What kinds of experiences did you have?
- How did they change your life from that of a Rough Ashlar?
- Thinking about it now, what else might you learn from that experience?

TWO

The Officers of the Lodge

As the Lodge and its accouterments represent the structure of the psyche, so the seven officers who serve within the Lodge represent the seven stages of psychological consciousness possible to an incarnate human being. Although it is customary and correct to think of these officers as a hierarchy, with some having control over others, we must also remember that no officer is more important that another; each stage of consciousness must be functioning and in the correct relationship to the others, if the incarnate individual is to realize his potential. On page 6, we saw the diagram of the Four Worlds—Physical, Psychological, Spiritual and Divine. The adjacent diagram shows the positions of the Officers of the Lodge in the context of the Tree of Life and the Four Worlds.

Our discussion will consider the Officers as they are found in the modern English lodges. American lodges use a different set of Officers to accomplish similar ends, most notably excluding the Inner Guard, whose duties are assigned to the Junior Warden.

The Tyler or Outer Guard may be associated with GRAMMAR,

the Art that establishes strict rules for structuring ideas in order to communicate them and record them in the physical world. The Tyler may be viewed as representing that part of the psyche which is in intimate contact with the physical body through the central nervous system. It is a "guard" in that it protects the psyche from being overwhelmed by stimuli from the physical world.

The Inner Guard may be associated with LOGIC, the Art that teaches rules for rational analysis—highly structured but entirely psychological. It may also represent what modern psychology

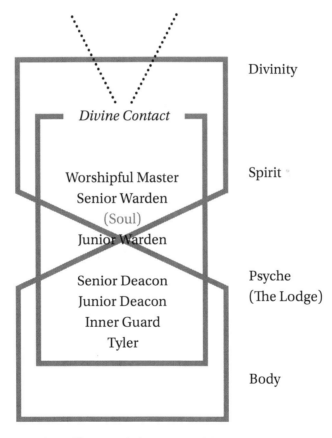

Lodge Officers and the Four Worlds.

refers to as the Ego, the habit-following executive of day-to-day psychological activity that is distinguished by its capacity to form mental images. It is a "guard" in the sense that it provides the persona that enables the psyche to relate to the world.

The Junior Deacon is associated with RHETORIC, the Art that teaches persuasive and impressive writing or speaking by invoking the feelings of the recipient. The Junior Deacon represents the feelings and moods, which, if examined, give clues to events that are happening in the unconscious. In the Classical world, Rhetoric also contained instruction in the Art of Memory, and the Junior Deacon also relates to the capacity to recall events from memory.

The Senior Deacon is associated with the Science of ARITHMETIC, a subject used for training in the manipulation and representation of abstract ideas. The Senior Deacon represents the level of Awakening. To be "awake" in this sense is to be present in the moment, to be aware of events as they occur both in the world and in one's psyche, to understand their implications, and to see the threats and opportunities they imply.

The Junior Warden may be associated with the Science of GEOMETRY, a "Science whereby we find the contents of bodies unmeasured by comparing them with those already measured."

The Junior Warden is similar to the Self in Jungian psychology. This somewhat obtuse Masonic definition of Geometry takes on greater meaning, when one realizes that it alludes to the old principle of "as above, so below." In the process of Masonic Labor, the Self is expected to emerge into consciousness and then to discover the contents of the unconscious through the observation of day-to-day experience.

The Senior Warden is associated with the Science of MUSIC, which had a much broader and mystical meaning for the Renaissance scholar that it does for us today. Music is based largely on the ratios between the frequencies of each note, the manner in which time is structured, and upon the way these are combined to produce specific effects. The Senior Warden can be seen to represent the level of the Soul; and the association with Music suggests the Soul's task of maintaining harmonious relationships among all the components of the psyche.

Worshipful Master may be associated with the Science of ASTRONOMY—which certainly included what we now call Astrology at the time our system was framed. As the observation of the heavens was thought to reveal the intentions of the Deity, Astronomy suggests a level of consciousness that can see at a broad, transpersonal scale, and can perceive the intent of the divine Plan. The level of consciousness represented by the Worshipful Master is in intimate contact with the Spirit.

CONTEMPLATIONS

- What does this tell you about the way Freemasonry can be understood in the context of your life?
- How can the study of the Seven Liberal Arts and Sciences expand your awareness of the lessons of Freemasonry? How might you make new progress in the study of these essential topics?
- How might you expand your knowledge of what each Officer is supposed to be and do?
- How might you relate each Officer and his responsibilities to your own, daily responsibilities?

THREE

The Three Great Lights

The candidate's status as an Entered Apprentice is confirmed by his obligation. The obligation requires only that he keep the secrets of Freemasonry. From the perspective we are using here, Masonry is a God-centered, developmental psychology, and in this context, secrecy is a container. Those involved in creative processes generally apply this principle to their work, holding it close until it is ready to be revealed, as a failure to do this can result in a loss of their energy. As the candidate works with the principles of the Craft, he will learn about the nature of himself and his relationship to the Universe and to divinity. These are intensely personal experiences, and secrecy is the container in which the individual preserves them.

For the early part of the Ceremony, the candidate is blind-folded, symbolizing his blindness as a natural man before moving through the threshold of consciousness. Once his obligation is complete, then he is restored to light, by having his blindfold removed, and the first things he sees are the Three Great Lights—the Square, the Compasses and the Volume of the Sacred Law. Their location in the Lodge indicates that, the reality they represent exists deep within the psyche of the individual. The Three Great Lights, together with the candidate who contemplates them, form a composite representation of Man as a miniature of the Universe as illustrated in the previous chapter.

The candidate's body represents the Physical World, as well as his own physical nature. The Square, the instrument concerned with form, represents the Psychological World, as well as the individual's psychological nature. The Compasses represent the Spiritual World, and the individual's spiritual being, and the Volume of the Sacred Law represents the divine World and contact with divinity.

In each degree, the arrangement of these Great Lights reflects the depth of awareness that characterizes the individual who has reached that level. The particular configuration of these symbols in the first degree indicates that the Entered Apprentice is conscious primarily at the level of his psychological nature. However, whenever they appear together, the arrangement of these Great Lights always emphasizes the fact that mankind and the entire Universe has its source in divinity.

CONTEMPLATIONS

- What do the concepts that we have described here mean for your daily life?
- How can you use this understanding of the Three Great Lights to enhance your work in the lodge?

FOUR

The Apprentice's Working Tools

T he Working Tools of the first degree are tools of action: the Gavel, the Chisel, and the Twenty-Four Inch Gauge.[1] From the Masonic perspective, these tools represent capabilities that the Entered Apprentice exercises many times each day.

The Gavel, which hits things hard, represents passion and we should note that this can include such emotions as joy, rage, and serious commitments of many sorts.

The Chisel, which when hit by the Gavel, has the capacity to direct passion in precise ways and to precise locations. In this manner it represents analysis, classification, and other forms of rational thought.

The Twenty-Four Inch Gauge, is an instrument of measuring, and it suggests that in employing the first two tools we should

---

[1] In the common American working, the Chisel is not included, although it is implied in the function of the Gavel. In the most widespread working used in England after 1816, the Working Tools of each degree are a triad. American Freemasonry represents older traditions that were not affected by changes in England resulting from the 1813 union of the Antients and the Moderns.

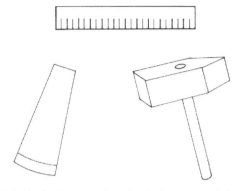

The Chisel, the Twenty-Four Inch Gauge, and the Gavel.

ensure that we keep them in balance. The number 24 also has an obvious reference to time, and to the ability to know "how much of each, and when."

The capacities of passion, analysis, and choosing/time-keeping are things which are done generally; and the Tools of the Entered Apprentice tell us that we can (and need to) think carefully about these activities, and to apply them to our daily life. We also need to understand the underlying principles and apply these activities to the Craft.

CONTEMPLATIONS

- What are the implications of this chapter for your daily life?
- Can you become aware of when you are using your Gavel? Do you generally over-use it, or under-use it?
- Can you become aware of when you are using your Chisel? Do you generally over-use it, or under-use it?
- Are you able to use the Twenty-Four Inch Gauge to balance the Gavel and Chisel and use them appropriately?
- Are you conscious of time, and the need for balance in your life?

CONTEMPLATING THE WAY OF THE FELLOW CRAFT

THE SECOND DEGREE IN PRACTICE

Since the symbolism of the Craft comprises a developmental psychology, the step to the second degree proceeds naturally as a result of progress in the First. This natural progression which relates to the gradual emergence of the Self is symbolized in this Degree by likening the new Fellow Craft to a ripened Ear of Corn—ready for the next stages in the maturation process that involve examining his interior psychological state. The Ear of Corn symbolizes the natural, unforced, psychological growth that has occurred as a result of the patient work in the first degree. Work at this next level occurs in a part of the psyche that is referred to in Masonic terms as the Middle Chamber, which is traditionally known as the Soul.

One of the key elements of the second degree tracing board is the Winding Staircase that describes seven levels of consciousness from consciousness of the physical body at the bottom, to consciousness of the Soul, Spirit and then finally divinity at the top. This is described in greater detail in the chapter on the Winding Stairs.

The winding staircase is flanked by two columns. These columns are opposite—active and passive—and the fact that they are introduced in the second degree relates them in some way to what Jung called the "personal unconscious," and to what is traditionally known as the Soul. They are said to be brass, cast in the clay ground—characteristics that related them to the physical world. They are also said to be hollow, containing the archives of the Craft. Taken together, these ideas of an archival record stored in the personal unconscious and relating to events in the physical world, suggest that the columns are a representation of an individual's memory, organized in such a way that memories that constrain and inhibit are found in one place, while those that enliven and move to action are found in another.

By introducing this idea here, in the Middle Chamber of the Soul, the symbolism indicates that the memories that are stored here are quite deep in the unconscious—not usually accessible—but available when one works at this level of consciousness.

As the individual climbs the Winding Staircase of consciousness and begins to work at the level of the Middle Chamber using the second degree Working Tools, the information that is stored becomes available to him so that he can examine these repressed memories which enables the emotional charge they carry to dissipate. He can examine them in the light of Justice, Mercy and Truth, discarding the constraints of conventional morality, and developing a higher and more balanced morality to guide his actions. Then those deep memories become ordinary memories, available for memory, but not carrying the emotional charge that can force or prevent behavior.

CONTEMPLATIONS

- What does the idea of maturing psychologically and developing the Soul mean to you?
- What kinds of characteristics of the Soul are different from those of the Ego or even the Self in the natural man?
- What additional capabilities and capacities are you likely to develop?

ONE

The Second Immovable Jewel: The Perfect Ashlar

As we saw earlier, the stone just cut from the rock is the Rough Ashlar, and in that form it is of virtually no use. The Rough Ashlar is associated with the Entered Apprentice, but the Perfect Ashlar is not associated with the Fellow Craft himself. Rather, the Perfect Ashlar is a stone made available in the Middle Chamber for the Craftsmen to try and adjust their tools on. The wooden tools lost their perfection with use, and as they measure by making comparison against absolute criteria, they needed to be recalibrated, so the Perfect Ashlar is a device for testing and recalibrating them. This is an important capability which carries substantial responsibility. It indicates that as one makes his own decisions and moral judgments he is expected to match his personal judgments with the standards of morality provided by the Deity in his own soul. Generally speaking one is expected to make these judgments in the context of his own religion.

CONTEMPLATIONS

- How can you match your personal judgments with the standards of divine morality?
- What are the implications of this chapter for your daily life?
- Of what kinds of things do you need to be aware?
- How can you use these insights?

TWO

The Winding Staircase

One of the key elements of the second degree tracing board is the Winding Staircase that describes seven levels of consciousness from consciousness of the physical body at the bottom, to consciousness of the Soul, Spirit and then finally divinity at the top. Each step on the Staircase is associated one of each of the seven Officers of the Lodge, and each of these Officers is associated with one of the Seven Liberal Arts and Sciences as described earlier. States of consciousness are difficult to describe, as they are arrived at by the individual himself experiencing shifts in his consciousness as he progresses up the Staircase, but the descriptions of the Officers and the Seven Liberal Arts and Sciences provide clues.

The Winding Staircase was part of King Solomon's Temple where it led to the Middle Chamber. The bottom of this staircase was guarded by the Junior Warden who required a password from those wishing to climb. The staircase consists of three, five, and seven (or more) steps. These numbers refer to the three Officers who rule a Lodge, to the five Brothers who hold a Lodge, and to the seven (or more) who make it perfect. The three who rule a Lodge are the Master and two Wardens, the five who hold a Lodge are the Master, two Wardens, and two Fellow Crafts. The seven who make it perfect are these five with two Entered Apprentices added.

Three rule a Lodge because at the building of King Solomon's Temple there were but three Grand Masters, Solomon, King of Israel; Hiram, King of Tyre, and Hiram Abif.

Five hold a Lodge in reference to the five noble orders of architecture, which are Tuscan, Doric, Iconic, Corinthian, and Composite. These orders of architecture are worth studying, as they deal with proportion, and the idea that temple buildings should incorporate proportions derived from the human form. This is based on the principle that man is a microcosm, the reflection of the universal macrocosm, and the image of divinity

Seven or more make a perfect Lodge because King Solomon was seven, or more, years building, completing, and dedicating the Temple to God's services. These seven years also relate to the seven liberal arts and sciences which are Grammar, Rhetoric, Logic, Arithmetic, Geometry, Music, and Astronomy. Remember that the new Fellow Craft is told that he is expected to make the liberal arts and sciences his future study.

CONTEMPLATIONS

- What are the implications of this chapter for your daily life?
- What can you learn from the concept of each of the steps, and the liberal art or science associated with each?
- What does it mean, in practice, to make the liberal arts and sciences your future study?
- Of what kinds of things do you need to be aware?
- How can you use these insights?

THREE

The Two Pillars

The Winding Staircase is flanked by two pillars which, taken together, are said to form a stable structure. These columns are complementary—active and passive—and the fact that they are introduced in the second degree relates them in some way to the psyche beyond the threshold of consciousness. They are said to be made of brass, cast in clay ground outside the Temple. Since the ritual in the first degree excludes metal, we might be surprised to find such prominent metallic structures here, and it suggests that whatever unconscious processes are to be associated with them, also relate to events that have occurred in the physical world. The Pillars are hollow to serve as archives of the Craft.

Since we are regarding the Temple as a representation of the new candidate's psyche, we can consider these Pillars, the archives, to be that part of his unconscious where his memories are stored. The memories that constrain and inhibit are found in the Passive Pillar, while those that enliven and move to action are found in the Active Pillar. By introducing this idea in the second degree, in the context of the Middle Chamber of the Soul, the symbolism indicates that the memories that are stored here are quite deep in the unconscious, not ordinarily accessible, but available when one works at this level of consciousness. Memories such as these are known to have a profound, although unconscious effect, on individuals and societies alike. At the individual level, they compel and inhibit a person's behavior, while at a social level, they define the society's concepts of morality. While circumscribed behavior is useful in causing people to fit into a family or society, especially during childhood, for adults it can be unproductively constraining and preventing of creativity. And social groups that believe that only their version of morality is appropriate, have often found themselves in bloody conflict with other groups with similar views.

This suggests that, as the individual climbing the Winding Staircase of consciousness begins to work at the level of his Soul, the information stored in these archives becomes available to him. As he brings these long-repressed memories into consciousness, he can examine them, decide whether they are still serving him, or not, and let the energy in them dissipate. This enables him to become more of his own person, more in possession of himself, and better able to make decisions based on more fundamental criteria, such as that to be described by the Working Tools in the next chapter.

CONTEMPLATIONS

- We can all remember "dos and don'ts" from childhood. Can you recall any don'ts that have had a profound impact on your life, and that may no longer be useful?
- Can you recall any dos that are still useful?
- Spend some time thinking about beliefs that were instilled

into you by your parents, teachers or religious figures.

- What beliefs about yourself do you recall? ("You're a great person," "You'll never make anything of yourself," "You're lazy," "You'll go far"...)
- Can you see how they have operated in your life?
- What beliefs do you still retain about the way society or its institutions work? ("Never trust a salesman," "Your teacher/preacher is always right," "Be good and you'll go to heaven," "Moncy docsn't grow on trees"....)
- How have they operated in your life? Do they serve you?

Contemplate all of these and decide which ones are still good and useful, and which you want to reject. In your thoughts and speech patterns, see how well you can do at giving them up.

FOUR

The Working Tools of the Fellow Craft

The first thing to observe is that, in contrast with the tools of action used by the Apprentice, the Working Tools of the Fellow Craft are tools of testing. All three of them test against absolute criteria. Two of the tools measure against criteria that are opposites and the third tool defines the relationship between the other two.

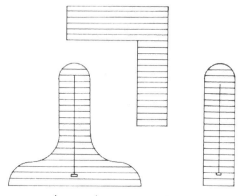

The Level, Square, and Plumb.

This looks like a system of morality; and if we follow that idea, we can assign some functional characteristics to the Working Tools. The Plumb Rule measures verticals; and in addition to the idea of "upright behavior," in the context of morality we can think of the idea of vertical as relating to our freedom of action, or to license. In contrast, the Level measures horizontals; and in addition to referring to "equality," we can think of the idea of horizontal as relating to our discipline or self-restraint, to rules that are to be followed. The Square, which defines the relationship between the Plumb Rule and the Level, can be thought of as our capacity to ensure that we apply license and restraint appropriately. That is certainly a good definition of "morality."

But there is a little bit more to this model. In the Middle Chamber we find the Perfect Ashlar "...for the experienced Craftsman to try his Jewels (which are the Fellow Craft's Tools) on." This is a wonderful image, probably from the operative Craft. The plumb rules, levels, and squares used by operative craftsmen were made of wood. We can understand that in the operative lodge a perfect ashlar would be maintained for the purpose of recalibrating the wooden plumb-rules, levels and squares that had been abraded by the stones on which they had been used. When we apply this idea of a "Perfect Ashlar" as a standard situated in one's Soul where it is used to calibrate the tools of morality it seems like a very good model of one's conscience.

This is an interesting model of morality, and it fits very nicely with the idea that within one's soul one has the capability to determine which things should be avoided, which things should be done, and how they should be done. When understood in this way, it is clear that the application of the Perfect Ashlar and the Working Tools of the Fellow Craft degree to our daily activities is of great importance.

CONTEMPLATIONS

- What are the implications of this chapter on morality for your daily life?
- What capabilities will the development and regular use of these tools give you?
- Of what kinds of things do you need to be aware?
- How can you use these insights in your daily life?

FIVE

The Position of the Square and Compasses

After the candidate confirmed his Obligation the Worshipful Master made reference to the Three Great Lights, and he pointed out that one of the points of the Compasses was now disclosed.

In an earlier chapter we indicated that the Three Great Lights refer to the Three Upper Worlds of divinity (Volume of the Sacred Law), Spirit (Compasses) and Psyche (Square), and in the Entered Apprentice Degree the Square, representing the, Psyche was on top; that is, it was dominant. Here in the Fellow Craft Degree the disclosure of part of the Compasses, representing the Spirit, symbolizes a rising in consciousness so that one can now be conscious of that influence.

The Square is used in four different contexts in Masonic ritual—and all of them refer to the Psyche. In the reception of the candidate, the Square represents one fourth of a circle. Since a circle is an almost universal symbol of the whole of existence, the fourth part of a circle makes reference to one of the four worlds. The purpose of the Square in the reception of the candidate is to inform him that the work of this Degree takes place entirely in the psyche, the Psychological World. And the manner of his reception also indicates that the candidate will be dealing with matters that relate to the heart.

The climbing of the Winding Stairs reflects the same advance. The Entered Apprentice Degree is held on the Ground Floor of the Temple which represents that level of consciousness that interfaces with the Physical World. At the top of the Winding Stairs the candidate is enabled to enter the Middle Chamber. The Middle Chamber is a very important place. It is a representation of the Soul; and as you will see, it is the seat of morality.

So the arrangement of the Square and Compasses is a very significant symbol.

CONTEMPLATIONS

- What are the implications of this chapter for your daily life?
- What does knowing that you are developing your heart and your Soul's capacities mean to you?
- What obligations do you incur? And how can you meet them?

SIX

The Password

The password for the second degree is derived from a Biblical event of some complexity. Since that event is quite unique, we will not make a detailed description of it here; because to do so might enable non-Masons to research the Scripture and identify the word. However, it is possible to discern the principles that this symbol communicates without focusing on too much of the detail.

We should start with the observation that this password is required before one can undertake the climbing of the Winding Stairs, and from that we can conclude that we must not undertake the mystical ascent (i.e. seek an elevated level of consciousness) without applying these principles to our own activities. The group which experienced severe difficulties in this Biblical story made two serious mistakes. First, they did not accomplish the activities that were prerequisite for what they desired. That is, they had not participated in a specific war, and as a result they were not entitled to partake of the spoils of that war. Second, they undertook their action with the wrong motive; they sought to take a part of the spoils to which they were not entitled.

How do these ideas apply to Freemasons seeking to start the mystical ascent? First, one must do the necessary prerequisites. From the Masonic point of view, that means that before one undertakes to rise in consciousness one must learn the necessary lessons. These are the lessons communicated in the first degree, and in this context learning these lessons means much more than simply being able to describe the teachings of the Entered Apprentice Degree. The lessons of the first degree must be incorporated into one's being; one must become the sort of person of which the first degree speaks. This includes the individuation of the "Self" as the phrase is understood in Jungian Psychology. That is why the questions at the end of the chapters are important.

Second, when one undertakes the mystical ascent one must have the proper motive. There are all manner of reasons why people seek to achieve an elevated level of consciousness. Some want to be able to read other people's minds and learn secret things for their own advantage. Others want to be able to perform magic and impose their will on the universe. Activities of this sort are very hazardous. From the Masonic point of view there is only one reason for seeking to rise in consciousness; and that is to reach the Middle Chamber of one's Soul and, ultimately, to experience the divine Presence.

If one applies these two principles of "proper preparation" and "proper motive" to one's own activities, one can anticipate a rich and rewarding journey.

CONTEMPLATIONS

- From what you have read in the earlier chapters related to the first degree, how can you incorporate the lessons into your life and being?
- What are the implications of the need for proper preparation for your daily life?
- Of what kinds of things do you need to be aware?
- Do you truly have the proper motive?

SEVEN

The Wages of a Fellow Craft

We are told that our ancient Brethren went to the Middle Chamber to receive their wages. As the wages were always fair, this is presented as a happy event; and beyond this mentioning, the symbol does not figure prominently in Masonic teaching as it is usually communicated today. However, when we consider the Middle Chamber in the context that we have introduced in these brief chapters the idea of wages is quite different. It suggests that in the Middle Chamber of our own being, our Soul which is the seat of our morality, there is an agency that ensures that we receive exactly what we deserve. From one perspective this can be a very cheerful idea; but from the point of view of a Brother who finds himself in a difficult or unpleasant situation it could be the sort of thing he does not want to hear. In fact, the symbol of wages is our Craft's device for teaching a very important and very fundamental principle: Each individual human being is the creator of his own experience. In the Western version of the Great Light this principle is communicated by the passage, "As a man soweth, so shall he reap."

There are two things to note about this principle when we are seeking to apply it to our own experience. The first thing is that this principle is the very foundation of individual freedom. It requires that we acknowledge that we are responsible for every situation in which we find ourselves. After we have done that—after we have stopped blaming others for our difficulties —if we do not like the situation we are in, we can change it. All we have to do is to "work in a different way," to "sow" differently. Now, sometimes our situation will not allow us to do very much differently. But the world is a system. Even if only a small thing can be done differently, the situation will change a little. In the changed situation something else can be done differently, and there will be other changes and other opportunities to do more things differently. It may take a good bit of time; but, eventually, significant changes to our personal situation can be achieved.

The second thing to note about this principle is that there are two dimensions to the way we "work" or "sow." The first of these dimensions consists of the things that we do to accomplish a task; and this is action, the dimension of sowing that is most generally recognized. The second of these dimensions is the attitude or frame of mind that we have while thinking about, and working on, that particular task. This second dimension is not generally recognized, but it is in many ways the more significant of the two. We sow by the way we think even more than by what we do; and if we can maintain a positive attitude toward a subject, we can expect to see a much more positive result.

The Symbol of Wages is not often discussed or appreciated; indeed, it is rarely mentioned at all. However, the effect of how we "sow" is very powerful. If the principles of the Symbol of Wages are applied properly, it can have a very profound and very positive impact on our lives.

CONTEMPLATIONS

- What are the implications of this chapter for your daily life?
- Of what kinds of things do you need to be aware?
- How can you use these insights?
- Some of these ideas are very subtle. They mean, for instance, that if you are angry, giving out an angry "vibe," then that is what you will attract back to yourself—that's why arguments can ratchet up and become stronger and more violent.
- If you give out feelings of love and kindness, then that's what you will attract.
- So what are you giving out most of the time?
- How can you learn to be more positive and kind?

CONTEMPLATING THE WAY OF THE MASTER MASON

THE THIRD DEGREE IN PRACTICE

The Master Mason's Degree is difficult to interpret because the ritual describes a psychological process which does not occur very frequently in our society. When it does occur, it is so intensely personal that few who have experienced it are prepared to discuss it with others, although with the increasing openness in society, especially among younger people, this is might be beginning to change.

This degree communicates a legend that is found in different forms in almost every human culture. The legend has two aspects: the first is of a primordial disaster, a catastrophic event that results in profound loss and imposes great hardship on Mankind; the second alludes to the means by which the loss can be made good and the original, blissful, human state restored. A slightly different version is the "Fall"—the expulsion of Adam and Eve from Eden, where they were in direct contact with the

Deity, and were sustained by God directly, and then found themselves on Earth, where they had to fend for themselves. In the Masonic treatment of this story, the events are described using the symbolism of Death.

The death of the architect described in the third degree is not physical death, but an individual psychological process that is in some way analogous to physical death. In this short introduction, it is not possible to write a detailed description of the events from the legend. But let us relate the principles contained in the legend to the individual human being who is heir to the processes of the "Fall." If we consider the individual to be the "Temple of God," then in one sense the building of that Temple is nearly completed when the individual is about to be born. The person who is destined to occupy the infant body has a Spirit, a Soul, and a Self; and he resides in Eden (in blissful contact with Divinity) until the time for his birth arrives and his body (his "coat of skin") is ready to receive him. In this context, the death of the Architect represents the event at the moment of birth when the Self (Junior Warden) is overwhelmed by the impact of confinement in the physical body and loses consciousness—particularly conscious contact with its Soul, Spirit and divinity. The "death" or restriction of consciousness reflects at the individual level the conscious separation from the Deity which the story of the "Fall" describes for mankind. In the Masonic legend, the Architect is described as being buried in a grave no larger than a man's body—limited in capacity for action or restraint. The legend also implied that the blissful, Edenic state that preceded the incarnation is possible only when all three Principal Officers (Self, Soul and Spirit) are operational. This makes it clear why the "secrets of a Master Mason" (the consciousness of the Upper Worlds) are lost.

The ritual of the third degree, as it is conducted in the Lodge, simply describes the process of the "death of the Self" in dramatic form; and in that way the ritual provides a sort of introduction to the subject. The actual event can occur only in people who are psychologically mature. Only a person who has assumed responsibility for his life, experienced the emergence of the Self, developed his own will, and is prepared to surrender it to the Deity, is "entitled to demand that last and greatest trial by which alone [he] can be admitted to the secrets of this [Master Mason's] degree." The wording of that quotation is important. The ritual is speaking of a psychological process; it will be difficult (a trial) and the individual must initiate the process himself (he is entitled to demand it,) and until this psychological process is allowed to occur, the individual's development will cease (it is the sole means of advancement.) The Lecture tells us that the real experience is accomplished "by the help of God," and we may assume that it occurs when the Deity wills it. When it does occur, it comes as do all Masonic initiations, in the context of the "ordinary duties of one's station in life."

For instance, the individual may find himself, in his ordinary life, in a situation of great difficulty, but one for which he has been trained, and with which he should be able to cope. As he works with the situation his abilities fail one by one. His analyses seem correct, but produce no useful answers; his actions, conducted on the basis of long experience, produce no useful results. Outside help is not available to him because his psychological situation prevents him from opening himself to those who could help him. Each time he turns to one of his carefully developed and trusted capabilities, it betrays him. A means of escape presents itself, but he rejects it because it involves the violation of some moral principle which he is committed to uphold. Instead, he perseveres; the external circumstances worsen; and his situation continues to deteriorate. At last, he turns to the "East," to the place in his being which experience has taught him is the source of unfailing help in time of desperate need ....

And it kills him.

What remains of him is buried in the rubble of the psychological Temple that he has built with such care.

Then the individual is raised from this grave of psychological rubble to find himself in a Master Mason's Lodge, in the Porchway Entrance to the Holy of Holies in the Temple which is his own being; and through its Veil he can glimpse the presence of divinity.

CONTEMPLATIONS

If you have been through this ceremony, what kind of impact did it have on you?

- Did any particular parts resonate with you and make you conscious that they had a deeper meaning?
- What can you learn by contemplating them?
- Have you had an experience in your daily life that seems like this experience of the third degree? Did it change you or your attitudes in any way?
- What do you think it means for you, personally, to experience the death of your Self?
- What will change about your life when you do experience the death your Self?

ONE

Approaching the East

I t is clear that the manner in which one takes the steps to approach the East in the Master Mason's degree makes reference to the subject of death and to getting past the issues which are involved with that subject. Indeed, that is the subject of this degree. Many brethren think of it in terms of physical death, and there are certainly useful thoughts in this area. However, when we look at the subject from the perspective that these short comments have represented, the issues are rather different.

Let us consider the following comment by W. Bro. Walter Leslie Wilmshurst in *The Meaning of Masonry*:

> Hence the third degree is that of mystical death, of which bodily death is taken as figurative, just as bodily birth is taken in the first degree as figurative of entrance upon the path of regeneration. In all the mystery systems of the past will be found this degree of mystical death as an outstanding and essential feature prior to the final stage of perfection or regeneration.[1]

1   W. L. Wilmshurst, *The Meaning of Masonry* (San Francisco, Calif.: Plumbstone, 2008), 98.

This is a very different perspective, framing the Craft in the context of ancient initiatic traditions of death and rebirth.

CONTEMPLATIONS

- On first reading, what does this subject mean to you?
- Up until now, have you only thought of this as a physical death?
- What different insights do you have, even before reading further?

TWO

Two Slips and a Grip

T he act of raising may be seen as representing the crossing of the threshold between the Psychological and Spiritual Worlds. To do so the candidate must die to his concept of himself as a Self (the essence of his psyche—as discussed earlier) in order to realize his identity as a spiritual being who possesses a Self, just as his Self possesses a body.

In the process of being raised to the degree of a Master Mason, the two Wardens, representatives of lower parts of the psyche, cannot accomplish this, but the Most Worshipful Master, representing the part of the psyche at the level of the Spirit, and in contact with divinity, accomplishes the task in conjunction with the Wardens. The Junior Warden attempts to raise the candidate with the . . . . . of an Entered Apprentice which proves a . . . . . In a like manner the Senior Warden attempts to raise him with the . . . . . of a Fellow Craft which has a similar result. The candidate is actually raised only when the Worshipful Master grasps his hand with the true . . . . . of a Master Mason. There is an important lesson to be learned from this series of events.

The teachings of the Entered Apprentice Degree and the skills that are derived from them are of great value, and they should certainly be applied whenever they relevant. But they apply to the activities in the physical world. In a like manner, the teachings of the Fellow Craft degree and the skills of morality derived from them are of even greater value; and they, too, should be applied with diligence. These skills also apply to activities in the physical world, and to some extent to the psychological world.

The lessons learned and the skills acquired while working at the levels of consciousness symbolized by the Entered Apprentice and the Fellow Craft degrees are of great value. However, as the failure of the ..... of these two degrees indicates, the teachings of those degrees do not relate to the level of consciousness symbolized by the Master Mason's degree. The third degree is an entirely different situation relating to the World of the Spirit, and the material taught at that level must be learned and applied in its own way.

At the level of the Spirit, the Master Mason has the ability to see all Four Worlds—and to work in them. This gives him a much larger picture of what is going on in his own life and the larger world about him, enabling him to be more detached from it than most, and able to make better decisions than he could from his day-to-day ego perspective.

CONTEMPLATIONS

- What are the implications of this chapter for your daily life?
- Of what kinds of things might you now become aware?
- Have you ever had a situation in which you have had such a larger perspective on a situation?
- What did it feel like?
- How can you use these insights?

THREE

The Posture for the Word

T he posture into which the candidate is raised, from a superficial flat to a lively perpendicular, is also the posture in which the Master Mason's word is communicated. This raising is, perhaps, the most significant event in Masonic ritual. It is a raising from a symbolic death; but the questions are: What is the nature of that death? What is it that dies? What is the nature of that raising? For some it is physical death and affirmation of life-after-death, but there are much richer interpretations.

Let us interpret a review the symbolism of the rituals. The prerequisite for starting the Masonic journey, the mystical ascent, was the individuation of the Self as defined in Jungian psychology. This "Self" is the individual free from the influences of others and making his own decisions, using his own values, and living his own life. His "Self" is a free-standing, responsible, independent human being; and it is this self-sufficient individual that was able to undertake the start of the mystical ascent by climbing the Winding Stairs. The candidate could not undertake such a task without that independence. In this way he was able to begin the journey in consciousness and to explore the Temple That He Is. What, then, is the nature and purpose of this ritual death?

Eventually, in his explorations, he reached that part of the Temple That He Is that is the Holy of Holies; and there was a difficulty. The Holy of Holies is that part of the Temple in which the Deity is to be found. The Deity has no limit, and when one becomes conscious of the presence of a Being that is without limit his Self cannot exist. It dies. That is the nature of the ritual death he has experienced. It is not physical death, it is not loss of identity, it is the death of the Self.

With the Self, and the intellectual concepts with which it is identified, out of the way the candidate was "raised" to a higher level of consciousness. The posture into which he was raised is that of oneness with the Worshipful Master. We can think of the WM as being a level of consciousness in contact with the World of the Spirit; and from that level one can be aware of the divine Presence. That awareness is the purpose of the mystical ascent.

CONTEMPLATIONS

- If you have been raised, what kinds of insights did you have during the ceremony?
- Did the ceremony resonate with you in any way, or give you a new understanding of Masonry or of Life?
- How can you use these insights?
- What are the implications of this process for your daily life?

FOUR

The Third Immovable Jewel: The Tracing Board

In the previous degrees, we have understood the work to be accomplished by the candidate from the perspective of the first two Immovable Jewels. The Rough Ashlar of the Entered Apprentice indicated the candidate becoming an individual and taking responsibility for himself. The Perfect Ashlar of the Fellow Craft indicated the presence within each human Soul of an internal, absolute, criterion against which the Fellow Craft must measure his morality. Both of these are concerned with personal development. The Immovable Jewel that relates to the Master Mason is not a stone, but the tracing board, said to be for the Master Mason to "draw designs on." The business of the third degree transcends personal considerations, and the designer has a substantial freedom of action to determine the form of the structure he will bring into being. The tracing board deals with the relationship between stones and with the whole larger structure to which they belong.

This idea of vastly increased scope of action is communicated directly by the configuration of the Great Lights in the third degree. The Compasses (representing the Spirit) are no longer constrained by the Square (representing the Psyche) as they have been in the previous degrees, and the person who has reached this level of consciousness is said to be "at liberty' to use the capabilities that the Compasses represent; to "render the circle of Masonic duties complete;' to operate consciously, in contact with all Four Worlds. This indicates that the concerns of a Master Mason are transpersonal and holistic.

CONTEMPLATIONS

- What does this chapter mean for you, in both your daily life and your Masonic life?
- What kinds of things might you do to develop the capability to see things more holistically and transpersonally?

FIVE

The Ornaments of the Lodge

I n the most common English working of the third degree, the Ornaments of a Master Mason's Lodge are the Porchway Entrance to the Holy of Holies (where the Master Mason's Lodge is said to meet), the Square Pavement of that Porch, and the Dormer Window which illuminates the Porch.[2] This collection of symbols, and particularly their placement close to the Holy of Holies, where divinity is said to reside, indicates that a Master Mason, in the sense that we are defining him, is a person who is conscious at a psychological level which relates to the World of the Spirit in the same way that our ordinary ego is conscious of the body and the physical world.

He stands on the Square Pavement which is the same symbol of duality and separation that we saw in the first degree but, in the divine Light that shines through the Dormer Window, he sees it differently. He sees that he, as a Master Mason walking on the Square Pavement, is to be a conscious bridge between all four worlds. He sees that the apparently independent objects

2   The Dormer Window was an early symbol, found in the work of the 1730s, which was retained in England, but is not used in the common American workings.

in the world are simply unique manifestations of divinity as It projects Itself into existence. And it harks back to an admonition that the newly raised Master received long ago. In a very real sense, the Master Mason is no more (and no less) than an individual whose responsibility it is to be conscious of that essential Unity, and to conduct "the ordinary duties of his station in life" in that consciousness—no matter how far the Masonic journey takes him.

As an additional perspective on the responsibilities of the Master Mason (not related to the Ornaments, but it is useful to mention it here) we see that he no longer aspires to the East. His orientation has changed, as indicated by the cardinal points on the third degree tracing board. He looks to the West from whence he has come in the attitude of the third of the Cardinal Virtues, Charity, which represents the frame of mind appropriate to the few who attain this Degree in fact, providing instruction to less experienced Brethren.

This environment of a Master Mason's consciousness may seem awesome, but the consideration of the Tools that are given to him to accomplish his work make us realize how important it is that he should have access to divine guidance, and how serious are the consequences of ignoring it.

CONTEMPLATIONS

- Can you imagine yourself as this "bridge between the four worlds?" What will that mean in practice?
- What does it mean to you to be aware of the Unity of all people and all things?
- In this context, what are "the ordinary duties of your station in life?"

SIX

The Working Tools of a Master Mason

T he Working Tools of the various degrees relate to the level of consciousness symbolized by each Degree. We have seen that the tools of the Entered Apprentice are Tools of Action, relating to the physical world. The tools of the Fellow Craft are Tools of Testing—testing against absolute criteria, relating to the business of morality. We have also noted that in each case two of these tools relate to "opposites" and the third tool keeps the first two in balance.

In the common American working, the Working Tools of this degree comprise all of the implements of stonemasonry,

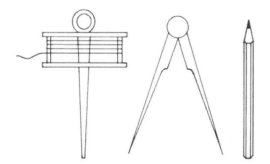

The Skirret, the Compass, and the Pencil.

with a special emphasis on the symbolism of the Trowel. In the working widely adopted in England after 1816, the Working Tools are a triad, just as in prior degrees: the Pencil, the Skirret, and the Compass.

In the hands of a Master Mason, these are Tools of Creativity, and creativity is the quality of the Spirit. The Pencil, the active tool, is a tool of design used to draw the plans and pictures which the architect or craftsman has in his head. We should note that when a picture is drawn it "changes worlds." That is, at first, as the architect is designing the structure the image exists as inspiration in his mind, in the psychological world. When the architect draws the picture and the plan with the pencil they exist in the physical world. We can think that the Pencil symbolizes inspired wisdom which exists initially in the World of the Spirit, and is received by the Master Mason in his mind as he opens himself to receive the inspiration.

By contrast the Skirret is a constraint on the pencil, and we can think that it symbolizes a principled understanding that enables the Master Mason to receive his inspired ideas, and organize them in a coherent format. As the Skirret enables the architect to place his pencil in exactly the right place to achieve his intent, so by his understanding the Master Mason is enabled to make coherent use of the inspiration he receives. We could even expand the definition of the Skirret to convey the idea of Laws, Traditions and Fundamental Principles.

The Compass is a mediating tool of consciousness, an instrument of proportion, and it enables the architect to coordinate and make appropriate the use of the other two tools. By the use of these tools of creativity the "designs"—inspired ideas and plans—that the Master Mason creates can be in accordance with the intention of the Great Architect.

As the Master Mason uses these tools and becomes proficient in them in his daily life, he will find that he becomes more creative and productive in all his endeavors, whether at home, at work or in the context of his Masonic life.

CONTEMPLATIONS

- Can you remember circumstances in which you have used one or more of these Working Tools in your daily life?
- Are there areas in your life where you could be more creative? More constraining? More balancing?
- How might you use these insights about the Working Tools?

SEVEN

East and West

There is one more idea upon which we should touch that is relevant for both the first and third degrees. A Mason is sometimes called a "traveling man," and one of the Masonic catechisms gives us a little insight into this seldom-used epithet:

> Q. Did you ever travel?
> A. My forefathers did.
> Q. Where have they traveled?
> A. East and West.
> Q. What was the object of those travels?
> A. They traveled East for instruction, and went West to propagate the knowledge they had obtained.

Notice the cardinal points of the compass on the Border of the first degree tracing board on page 9. They define the East West direction as it is to be understood in terms of Masonic Symbolism, and in doing so they make some comment about the nature of the journey which the new Mason apprentices himself to undertake. That journey from West to East is represented, symbolically, by the progress through the Masonic degrees; and it is, in fact, the ascent up Jacob's Ladder, one of the "Principal Rounds" for each Degree.

Indeed, from the point of view from which we are speaking, the "East-West Dimension" as shown on the tracing boards is the dimension of consciousness: ordinary consciousness of the physical world at the West and consciousness of the divine Presence at the East. As we have seen, the notion of a "mystical ascent" was part and parcel of the Hermetic / kabbalistic Tradition. It is a devotional exercise, conducted in the context of the religious belief of each individual, during which the individual rises through the worlds of the soul and the spirit and at last finds himself experiencing the presence of the Deity. As he starts on the interior journey the Mason is inexperienced. He must depend upon his interior guidance, that is, he must practice the first of the Cardinal Virtues: Faith. As depicted on the tracing board of the first degree, the allegorical figure of Faith is associated with the Volume of the Sacred Law and the lower rungs of Jacob's Ladder. Only by Faith may we approach the sacred mystery at the heart of the Masonic experience.

The allegorical figure of Hope occupies the medial rungs of the Ladder. The Cardinal Virtue of Hope inspires perseverence. The work of ascent is challenging, and this she signifies the perseverence that each aspirant must maintain along the path towward the Light.

Finally, after being raised in the third degree, the Master Mason's orientation has changed, as indicated by the cardinal points of the compass on the tracing board. The Master Mason looks back toward the West from which he has come in the attitude of the third Cardinal Virtue: Charity. The allegorical figure of Charity stands on the highest of the principal rungs of Jacob's Ladder, in the part of the first degree Board that represents the psyche, but with her head in the area representing the Spirit, and illumined by the Glory of divinity. She nurses a child, symbolizing the Master Mason's responsibility to nurture those who follow him.

CONTEMPLATIONS

- Thinking about the Faith that you had as you started the Masonic journey—what assisted you and kept you on that journey?
- Now that you have completed the journey and are facing back to the West, what can you do to nurture those Masons who are following you?
- What specific guidance would you want to impart to them?
- How can you develop a conscious intent to do that?

THE LODGE AS
A WORKING
GROUP

The prime focus in this book has been the individual, working his way through the degrees to attain a higher level of consciousness. In this section, we will touch on another principle, but infrequently observed, aspect of the Lodge—a group of people working to apply the principles of Freemasonry to their own experience and to realize, in their own consciousness, the levels of awareness symbolized by the degrees. Because this aspect of the Craft can be intensely personal, this description of practical work is brief, but we can outline some general principles which, if carefully followed, will lead the serious Apprentice to a situation in which he can undertake more formal work.

Generally speaking, one does not undertake interior work alone. Monasteries provide support for those who want to devote themselves completely to this pursuit. However, generally, the traditional form of study in the western world, is a group that meets periodically to contemplate some body of philosophical text or scripture. Typically, in such a group, each member in turn reads a paragraph, after which the members discuss the implications of the text, analyze the principles it contains and, if possible, give examples of the operation of those principles in their own experience. This sharing of experience and perspective among the members of the group provides each with a richer insight into the text and to its application in his own life than he might otherwise have had. In a similar way, the recognition of the principles working in another's life can assist one to see them operating in one's own. On occasion, this process can cause substantial emotional distress; for example, an individual might see his own behavior in a new light and realize that he has hurt many people in the past. In such a situation, membership in the group can be a source of real emotional support during the period of crisis.

The text that the group studies serves two purposes. First, it provides the context and the subject matter for the discussions; and second, it provides a link through the teachings of Freemasonry to the "philosophical teaching" which is the property of the race of man. If the group is fortunate, it will have a tutor (generally the Worshipful Master) who will be able to draw out the contributions of the individual members, and enrich the discussions with perspectives that would otherwise not be available. Such a tutor is usually only one step ahead of the other members. He may be attracted to the lodge because of its interests, or one of the members may develop into the role because of his understanding and ability to work with people. In either case, the position of tutor carries great responsibility because the other members of the group will have placed the guidance of their interior development in his hands, and if not careful, he could do them psychological damage. The role of tutor to a working group requires the greatest personal integrity;

and as a rule of thumb, it may safely be said that the desire for the position is an automatic disqualification.

A group working in the way outlined above is following the Way of Contemplation; that is, using the analytical faculty as a means to understand the teaching. While this is quite a common approach in the West, as it fits with the western temperament, and requires nothing besides the text, it is not the only way of study. A group that meets for prayer and meditation is following the Way of Devotion and this, too, is a common approach that can be practiced with great simplicity. There is a third approach— the Way of Action—and this approach is used by groups that use ritual as their means of practicing their tradition. Clearly the Masonic Lodge makes use of all three of these methods, sometimes, with a little more emphasis on ritual.

The parallel between the Masonic Lodge and the traditional working group is quite clear. The balanced combination of action, contemplation and devotion appears to have been the original concept of formal Masonic Labor, and any Lodge or Masonic study group that undertakes such a curriculum seriously will find itself amply rewarded. In the usual course of events, very few Masons give their attention to the Lodge in its capacity as a working group.

Indeed, such Lodges are quite rare at the present time. There are some however, of which I am aware, in the United States and the United Kingdom, and to visit one is a worthwhile experience. To be a member of one is a real privilege. In the United States and Canada, many such lodges describe themselves as Traditional Observance, meaning that they endeavor to follow the traditional approach to Freemasonry as a serious and contemplative Craft. Lodges of many kinds are focusing more intently upon Masonic education, and opportunities for a more profound engagement with the Craft's inner teachings are becoming more available.

INDIVIDUAL LABOR
IN THE CONTEXT OF THE WORKING GROUP

Each member of the Working Group has responsibilities to ensure that it operates productively. First, learn the Ritual. Not only is this important from the perspective of the Lodge, but it helps the individual to exercise those psychological functions symbolized by the Gavel (repetitive action) and the Chisel (communication.) Then participate in the Ritual whenever possible. This requires being psychologically awake—at the place where the Psychological and Spiritual Worlds meet. This makes one receptive to the deeper meaning that is implicit in the Ritual and Symbols—so that the whole Ritual is conducted consciously rather than by rote.

Make use of the Opening and Closing. Since the Lodge is a model of the individual psyche that has at its center a contact with divinity, the Ceremony of Opening represents opening one's consciousness to that divine Center, and then Closing it again with reverence.

The Ceremony starts when the Master knocks and then the Tyler presents himself and is posted. A similar process posts the Inner Guard. This fragment of the Ritual symbolizes the process by which one makes one's self secure from interruptions, and turns one's Ego consciousness from the concerns of the Physical World to the Temple within (symbolized by the Lodge.) With the Temple secure, the Master names each Officer and reviews his duties. This recalls and activates each level of consciousness in turn. Then before opening the Lodge, the Master invokes the blessing of the Deity. This takes only a moment, but it is of critical importance. No one should undertake interior work without divine Permission; and if, for some reason, that permission is withheld, the Lodge should not be opened. Only after the assurance of the approbation of the Deity does the Master open his Lodge and start the labor of the evening.

In order to use this Ceremony in one's own individual work, one should set aside a period each day for devotion and meditation; open that period by reciting the Ceremony of Opening, make such prayers and meditations as one's conscience and religion direct, and then close the period with the Ceremony of Closing.

In addition, familiarize yourself with the Lectures and the material to which they refer. Learn to draw the basic images of the tracing board of each Degree. Practice until you can draw them from memory, and as you draw them, review in your mind the principles that are represented by the various objects as they are discussed in the lectures. Remember that those principles are operating within you and the world every day. Observe their operation and understand what is happening to you and in you.

Finally, remember the Lodge at regular intervals. This is a very old practice among groups involved in philosophical work, and it has various benefits. For the individual it is another practice of remembering (and using the Gavel and Chisel.) For the Group it is much more. The Lodge, as everything in the relative Universe, exists in all Four Worlds; and by calling the Lodge into consciousness and thinking about it, one invests psychological energy in it, and it becomes 'sharper' at the psychological level. There are a few Lodges whose members have practiced this remembrance diligently for many years through a Lodge prayer said at noon every day, while recalling all the Brethren. Entering such a Lodge is an unforgettable experience—visitors sense the 'atmosphere' and never fail to comment on it.

Remember that as a Freemason each individual is building a Temple to God. He is building an edifice in consciousness in which he, himself, is an individual stone.

CONTEMPLATIONS

- If we so desire, how might we form such a working group in our Lodge?
- What would we need to do to start?
- What kind of ground-rules would we need?
- How would we select a 'tutor'?
- What materials should we use to read and contemplate? Ritual or books by learned Masons?
- Would it be useful to have a Lodge Prayer?
- What can you, do, as an individual to enhance your experiences of working in the Lodge?
- What practices can you commit to on a daily basis?

CONCLUSIONS

The preceding chapters give a picture of a Master Mason who can be considered mature in the context of the developmental psychology we have developed from the symbols of Craft Freemasonry.

There may be temptations to resist using some of the methods that are described here, especially those of the third degree, as they may appear too lofty, requiring a more elevated consciousness than most individuals appear to have. But remember that these methods are functions of the psyche and they operate continuously (albeit sometimes unconsciously) in every individual. The question is not whether to use the methods, but whether to use them consciously and in the service of divinity.

The working group, described in the last section, can help with understanding and practicing the Craft at an individual level in individual life. The members of the working group should receive the guidance of the tutor with tentative acceptance, but should verify the guidance through their own experience.

The real Master Mason has a responsible and often lonely job, but he has the ability to call for help when he needs it. He can call on the "Sons of the Widow," a group taking its name from the physical world, the "Mother Earth," cut off and widowed from the divine connection by the events described as the Fall. (In other traditions, these people have been called "Blessed Company of Saints," or the "House of Israel.") The Craftsman comes from the West, seeking instruction. The Master Mason comes from the East, seeking that which was lost or cut off. They are both traveling the dimension of consciousness, and the goal is to reconnect and repair the loss.

So the Master Mason is one who stands in the light of divinity, with his feet on the ground of the everyday world, and recognizes the unity—the single, integrated manifestation—of divine Will through all the worlds. The development of such individuals is the real purpose of the Craft—making good men better.

CONTEMPLATIONS

- Do these ideas resonate with you? If so, how?
- What more can you do to develop yourself into a Master Mason in fact—not just as a titular rank?
- What can you do to assist in making good men better.

FURTHER
READING

FREEMASONRY

C.R. Dunning, Jr.
Contemplative Masonry (Stone Guild, 2016)

Colin Dyer
Symbolism in Craft Freemasonry (Lewis Masonic, 1976)

W. Kirk MacNulty
*The Way of the Craftsman: A Search for the Spiritual Essence
    of Craft Freemasonry* (Deluxe Edition, Plumbstone, 2017)
Freemasonry: A Journey Through Ritual and Symbol
    (Thames and Hudson, 1991)
Freemasonry: Symbols, Secrets, Significance
    (Thames and Hudson, 2006)

Angel Millar
Freemasonry: Foundation of the Western Esoteric Tradition
    (Salamander and Sons, 2016)

Freemasonry: A History (Thunder Bay Press, 2006)

Christopher B. Murphy, Editor
Exploring Early Grand Lodge Freemasonry: Studies in Honor
  of the Tricentennial of the Establishment of the Grand
  Lodge of England (Plumbstone, 2017)

Alexander Piatigorsky
Who's Afraid of Freemasons? The Phenomenon of
  Freemasonry (The Harvill Press, 1997)

Marsha Keith Schuchard
Restoring the Temple of Vision: Cabalistic Freemasonry and
  Stuart Culture (Brill, 2002)

David Stevenson
The Origins of Freemasonry: Scotland's Century, 1590–1710
  (Cambridge University Press, 1988)

Kirk White
Operative Masonry: : A Manual for Restoring Light and
  Vitality to the Fraternity (Five Gates Publishing, 2012)

W. L. Wilmshurst
The Meaning Of Masonry (Plumbstone, 2007)
The Masonic Initiation (Plumbstone, 2007)
The Ceremony of Initiation (1932; CreateSpace, 2013)
The Ceremony of Passing (1932; CreateSpace, 2016)

LIBERAL ARTS AND SCIENCES

Miranda Lundy and Anthony Ashton
*Quadrivium: The Four Classical Liberal Arts of Number,
Geometry, Music, & Cosmology* (Wooden Books, 2010)

John Michell and Rachel Grenon
*Trivium: The Classical Liberal Arts of Grammar, Logic, &
Rhetoric* (Wooden Books, 2016)

NEOPLATONISM

Proclus
A Commentary on the First Book of Euclid's Elements,
translated, with introduction and notes, by Glenn
R. Morrow (Princeton University Press 1970)

Pauliina Remes
Neoplatonism (University of California Press, 2008)

Fabio Venzi
The Influence of Neoplatonic Thought on Freemasonry
(Book Guild Publishing, 2007)
Freemasonry: The Esoteric Tradition
(Lewis Masonic, 2016)

Arthur Versluis
*Platonic Mysticism: Contemplative Science, Philosophy,
Literature, and Art* (State University of New York
Press, 2017)

KABBALAH

Arthur Green
A Guide to the Zohar (Stanford University Press, 2003)

Daniel C. Matt
The Zohar: Pritzker Edition (Stanford University Press,
2003–2017)

Z'ev ben Shimon Halevi
Kabbalah: Tradition of Hidden Knowledge (1980)
The Kabbalistic Tree of Life (2013)

HERMETICISM

Brian P. Copenhaver
*Hermetica: The Greek Corpus Hermeticum and the Latin
Asclepius in a New English translation*
(Cambridge University Press, 1992)

Clement Salaman, et al.
*The Way of Hermes: New Translations of The Corpus
Hermeticum and the Definitions of Hermes Trismegistus
to Asclepius* (Inner Traditions, 2000)

THE RENAISSANCE

Giovanni Pico della Mirandola
Oration on the Dignity of Man: A New Translation and
    Commentary, edited by Francesco Borghesi, et al.
    (Cambridge University Press, 2016)

Solomon Ibn Gabirol
The Font of Life (Fons Vitæ), translated by John A. Laumakis
    (Marquette University Press, 2014)

Angela Voss
Marsilio Ficino (North Atlantic Books, 2006)

Frances Yates
The Occult Philosophy in the Elizabethan Age
    (Routledge, 2003)
The Rosicrucian Enlightenment (Routledge, 2001)

About the Author

W. Kirk MacNulty was born in California in 1932. He studied at Stanford University and the University of Tennessee, and had a career in the United States Marine Corps and in corporate information technology.

His interest and involvement in Freemasonry spans more than fifty-five years. He received the degrees of Masonry in 1961 at Carson Valley Lodge № 33 of Gardnerville, Nevada. He later affiliated with lodges in Hawaii, Tennessee, England, and Virginia. He was Worshipful Master of the Lodge of Living Stones № 4957 in Leeds, England, in 1979, 1980, and 1991.

He is the Charter Master (1997) and current Tiler of the Lodge of the Nine Muses № 1776, a Traditional Observance Lodge in the District of Columbia.

In addition to *Contemplating Craft Freemasonry*, he has published *Freemasonry: A Journey Through Ritual and Symbol* (Thames & Hudson, 1991), *Freemasonry: Symbols, Secrets, Significance* (Thames & Hudson, 2006), and *The Way of the Craftsman: Deluxe Edition* (Plumbstone, 2018). His work has also appeared in *Heredom: The Journal of the Scottish Rite Research Society* and *Ars Quatuor Coronatorum*.

Bro∴ MacNulty's literary efforts have earned outstanding recognition. In 2008, he was received as a member of London's prestigious Quatuor Coronati Lodge № 2076, the world's premier lodge of research. In 2016, he was recognized as a Fellow of the Philalethes Society for his many contributions to the literature of the Craft.

THE · GEORGE · WASHINGTON
MASONIC · NATIONAL · MEMORIAL

*To inspire humanity through education
to emulate and promote the virtues,
character, and vision of George Washington,
the Man, the Mason, and Father of our Country.*

Open 9 a.m. to 5 p.m. seven days a week,
excluding major holidays.

Guided Tours Daily
9:30 a.m., 11:00 a.m., 1:00 p.m., 2:30 p.m. *&* 4 p.m.

101 Callahan Drive · Alexandria, Virginia
703-683-2007 · *www.gwmemorial.org*

Also from Plumbstone

The Way of the Craftsman:
A Search for the Spiritual Essence of Craft Freemasonry
W. Kirk MacNulty

Contemplating Craft Freemasonry:
Working the Way of the Craftsman
W. Kirk MacNulty

Exploring Early Grand Lodge Freemasonry:
Studies in Honor of the Tricentennial of
the Establishment of the Grand Lodge of England
Edited by Christopher B. Murphy *&* Shawn Eyer

The Meaning of Masonry
Walter Leslie Wilmshurst

The Masonic Initiation
Walter Leslie Wilmshurst

Sing the Art Divine:
A Traditional Masonic Songster
Nathan St. Pierre *&* Shawn Eyer

Ahiman: A Review of Masonic Culture & Tradition
Edited by Shawn Eyer

Freemasonry in the Wild West
Kyle A. Grafstrom

Masonic Perspectives:
The Thoughts of a Grand Secretary
Thomas W. Jackson

Made in the USA
Middletown, DE
02 October 2023

39952621R00066